40
Ideas
for
POSITIVE
THINKING

Damrong Pinkoon

Positive thinking is a starting point for **happiness.**

Happiness is a **starting point** for **success.**

Before thinking about *changing* anything Change your own *thought* process first.

One **positive point** of **human beings** is that their **thoughts** can be **developed.**

Many human beings want to change their surroundings and yearn to have the ideal life.

This makes people suffer unconsciously. The essence of a happy life does not depend on... being fulfilled with what we think we should get.

Rather the essence of living a happy life is to take action by doing the right things.

Those who live with unhappiness tend to experience continual problems in life.

These problems do not occur accidentally but, instead they derive from a pattern of negative thinking which accumulates relentlessly to drag suffering into life.

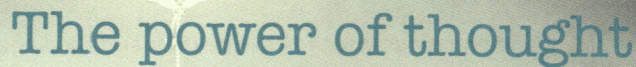

The power of thought

is endless

but **it can stifle life**

if developed in a negative way.

Mr. Positive is taught to be appreciative of other people

Mr. Negative is taught to look down on other people

★ ★ ★ ★ ★ ★ ★ ★ ★ ★ ★ ★ ★ ★ ★ ★ ★

Mr. Positive is taught to be kind to people

Mr. Negative is taught to be deceitful to people

★ ★ ★ ★ ★ ★ ★ ★ ★ ★ ★ ★ ★ ★ ★ ★ ★

Mr. Positive is taught to admire a good person

Mr. Negative is taught to admire a rich person

★ ★ ★ ★ ★ ★ ★ ★ ★ ★ ★ ★ ★ ★ ★ ★ ★

Mr. Positive is taught to speak, think and act in a proper way

Mr. Negative is taught to be an envious ruffian

★ ★ ★ ★ ★ ★ ★ ★ ★ ★ ★ ★ ★ ★ ★ ★ ★

Mr. Positive is taught to identify what is right and wrong

Mr. Negative is taught not to be able to identify what is right and wrong

★ ★ ★ ★ ★ ★ ★ ★ ★ ★ ★ ★ ★ ★ ★ ★ ★

Mr. Positive is taught to listen to the opinions of others

Mr. Negative is taught to disregard the opinions of others

★ ★ ★ ★ ★ ★ ★ ★ ★ ★ ★ ★ ★ ★ ★ ★ ★

Mr. Positive is taught to do good things when opportunity allows

Mr. Negative is taught to take advantage whenever opportunity allows

★ ★ ★ ★ ★ ★ ★ ★ ★ ★ ★ ★ ★ ★ ★ ★ ★

Mr. Positive is taught not to harm others

Mr. Negative is taught to betray others if chance allows

In the changing of thoughts
or lifting the thought level

from a child to a teenager to an adult, there occur changes called

"PARADIGM SHIFTS" (attitude).
When the PARADIGM SHIFTS

happen or attitudes change,
all our perceptions are changed too.

Today, people are
trapped with thoughts

caused by incorrect ways of learning,
trapped with irrelevant knowledge

caused by brainless programs,
trapped with warped intellects

caused by thoughts of materialistic gain and fame.

All these factors create confusion between suffering
and true happiness.
One desires an expensive car
but is not willing to pay the high cost of petrol.
One desires reconciliation with a partner but is afraid to lose face.
One desires fast food but is afraid to gain weight.

These confusing conflicts are called PARADOX THINKING
and they indicate that we fail to spend our daily lives in a balanced way.

We want to have positive thoughts and be mindful of others,
but we experience negativity all the time throughout our lives.

There are 40 easy ways to create positive thinking in life,

ways that will make you truly happy and alleviate suffering.

40 IDEAS FOR POSITIVE THINKING

IF YOU SPEND YOUR TIME AS IT IS THE FIRST DAY, YOU WILL HAPPY EVERYDAY.

Damrong Pinkoon

This book introduces

40

easy ways to create

positive
thoughts

that can be
simply applied
in daily life.

01

Find Good Experiences for Yourself

Nature creates systematic thoughts in us
but we artificially distort our own thoughts.
Those who have simple thoughts tend to find happiness more easily,
while those who have complicated thoughts tend
to have difficulty finding happiness.

Those who are unattached to a materialistic
lifestyle tend to have a carefree happiness,
while those attached to materialism become unhappy
when they lose their possessions.

Nature created us to share happiness together.
Nature also created us to be jealous
when seeing others better off than ourselves.

Nature created us to live together in societies
and to help one another.
Nature also created us to blame others when things go wrong.

One thing that many people fail to do is greet and smile to themselves.

38% of men wake up and then go to the toilet
42% of women wake up and go to the toilet

15% of men wake up and immediately brush their teeth
34% of women wake up and immediately brush their teeth

5% of men wake up and take a drink of water
1% of women wake up and take a drink of water

8% of men wake up and immediately watch television or listen to the radio.
1% of women wake up and immediately watch television or listen to the radio.

76% of smokers have a cigarette before breakfast

Not many people greet themselves
in front of the mirror every morning by saying...

"Hello"
"Hey…hey…hey…hello"
"Hello, handsome man"
"Hi…pretty girl"

Try to say this as you look at the person in the mirror
with an ugly face, messy hair, bad breath and wrinkles.
Don't be frightened because you are trying to change that face
to be beautiful and attractive.

(Who else will dare look at your face in such as state if not you?)

Human beings can be categorized into

4 types

> Group 1 : I am wrong and you are wrong.
> Group 2 : I am wrong but you are right.
> Group 3 : I am right but you are wrong.
> Group 4 : I am right and you are right.

Group 1: Self-blaming and blaming others

This is a person that has a negative attitude and tends to look down on him or herself, with the perception that they don't have the ability to do things. They think that others are unable to do things as well. This negative type of person, apart from looking down on others, is indecisive, they blame themselves and lack the courage to face the truth. Thinking like this every day is a sure fire way of making negative things become true in life.

Group 2: Self-blaming but appreciating others

This group of people has been raised with an inferiority complex. The feelings of inferiority have been caused by constantly being blamed by their parents or relatives from an early age. Whatever they did, it was usually perceived as wrong. Hence feelings of inadequacy have been imprinted on them. That they are "not good enough", "not smart enough", "not worth it". Thus, a lack of self-confidence has been established in them by adults. However, they are not entirely negative thinkers since they can still see the positives in others and some of the beauty in the world.

Group 3: Self-appreciation but blaming others

These people have more negative thoughts than people in the second group. He or she keeps an eye on what others do everyday, picking on other people, looking down on them and criticizing them. They readily blame their partner and children when things don't go right. At the end of life, this type of this person often ends up lonely without any friends. And if they do have a few friends, those friends are often of a similar negative type.

Group 4: Self-appreciation and appreciating others

This group of people is blessed with a beautiful view of the world. From an early age their parents taught them to have a positive view of life. Firstly, they were given good things in life. Secondly, they were taught to live with nature, to love the environment and animals. Thirdly, they were taught to identify between what is good and bad. And, more importantly, how to deal with the negativity that life throws up. Fourthly, they were taught how to solve problems without resorting to violence or harm. Finally, they were taught to appreciate the people around them. Their parents gave them good role models to follow and to live up to. And since these life lessons were taught from an early age, this group of people have grown up with positive, happy thoughts.

In terms of our children, we can instill positivity in them gradually in a number of ways, from watching movies, listening to music and through playing games...

Blaming or scolding is not a good way to create positive thoughts...

Teaching should be positively constructive as children grow up, not based on being furious, or showing intolerance and loathing.

This is important because adults tend to do things unconsciously and emotionally and before they become aware of what they have done, it can be too late.

> If we start with a good life,
> **our life will be good.**
> If we want to have a better life,
> We should think
> of everything in
> a positive way.
>
> Thinking positively,
> speak about positive things,
> emphasize good things everyday
>
> and this will enhance **a good life.**

WHICH IS YOUR FACE EVERY MORNING ???

> **Whom would you rather talk to...**
>
> **a person who looks displeased**
> or **a person who looks strained**
>
>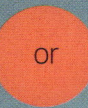
>
> would you rather not talk
> to either of them
>
> **???**
>
> *(Then think... do you tend to look displeased or strained?)*

02

Find Good Things for Yourself

If you spend your work life using heavy thought
processes everyday, you should get your brain
ready for a day's hard work
by doing some meditation.

An electroencephalogram (EEG) can measure the workings
of our brain waves.

There are 4 types of brain waves:

1). BETA waves *with a frequency of 14 - 30.0 Hz:*
In situations of learning + working + daily life (if having more serious
considerations, the frequency can climb to more than 30 Hz.

2). ALPHA waves *with a frequency of 8 - 13.9 Hz:*
In situations relating to happy children and adults with trained minds
(in a comfortable state).

3). THETA waves *with a frequency of 4 - 7.9 Hz:*
In situations of sleep or being heavily relaxed, highly trained minds,
advance concentration and positive thinking creating intellectual
and high creativity.

4). DELTA waves *with a frequency of 0.1- 3.9 Hz:*
In situations of deep sleep without dreams or advance meditation at the
level of Jhana (the highest concentration level in meditation).

Learning to know our own mind or
train our mind
is not a supernatural thing.
Good mind training allows one to
control emotions
and **thought processes.**

Training the mind lets us know
the art of living life,by learning
to use conscious senses to solve problems smartly.
The brain can be taught to be more creative
in work and in daily life.

This is because our **brain** has unlimited
memory storage, unlike a **hard disk.**
And our brain processes creative thought faster than any
computer.

Concentrating the mind in the morning
before going to work,or before going to bed
can make for a **happier life.**
**We can use our brain
to think deliberately
before doing anything.**

"

Some meditate aiming to
go to paradise after death.

However,
most positive thinkers aim
to develop concentration in
order to create
consciousness.

"

03

Find Good Things for Yourself

Our brains perceive based on the five senses
            Our eyes   - sense sight
            Our ears   - sense sound
            Our nose   - senses smells
         Our tongue   - senses flavors
Our hands and skin - give touch and texture

When we perceive any stimulus through the five senses,
the experience is recorded in our brain.
And these experiences can be recalled
as memories as and when we need them.
Occasionally, we might not want those memories
but they emerge just the same.

Someone's favorite song might be a melancholy air.
Whenever he or she listens to that song, he or she feels
broken-hearted and moved emotionally.
Some have a cheerful tune as their favorite song,
they feel euphoric when they hear it and want to dance.
The song has the ability to make them happy.

The beginnings of positive thinking
starts with the recording of
positive thoughts.

If we perceive bad things every morning,
the brain ends up filled with negative thoughts
which causes a generally unhappy life.

Similar to a malfunctioning computer affected by a virus,
the human brain can be polluted by negative thoughts.

If we constantly misbehave,
if we constantly do the wrong thing,

Such negativity perpetuates bad behavior.

Hence, when negativity occurs in your life,

you have no one else to blame but yourself.

Suppose that there are
two people living a similar lifestyle
but they do certain things differently.

The first person wakes up in the morning and watches a fun movie and later listens to a happy song before going to bed.

The second person wakes up in the morning and listens to broken-hearted songs and later watches violent movies before going to bed.

Are the lives of these two people so different?

Not really, only their tastes differ to a certain degree.

But good things tend to happen to the first person while the second person is more prone to

negative thinking

and unhappiness.

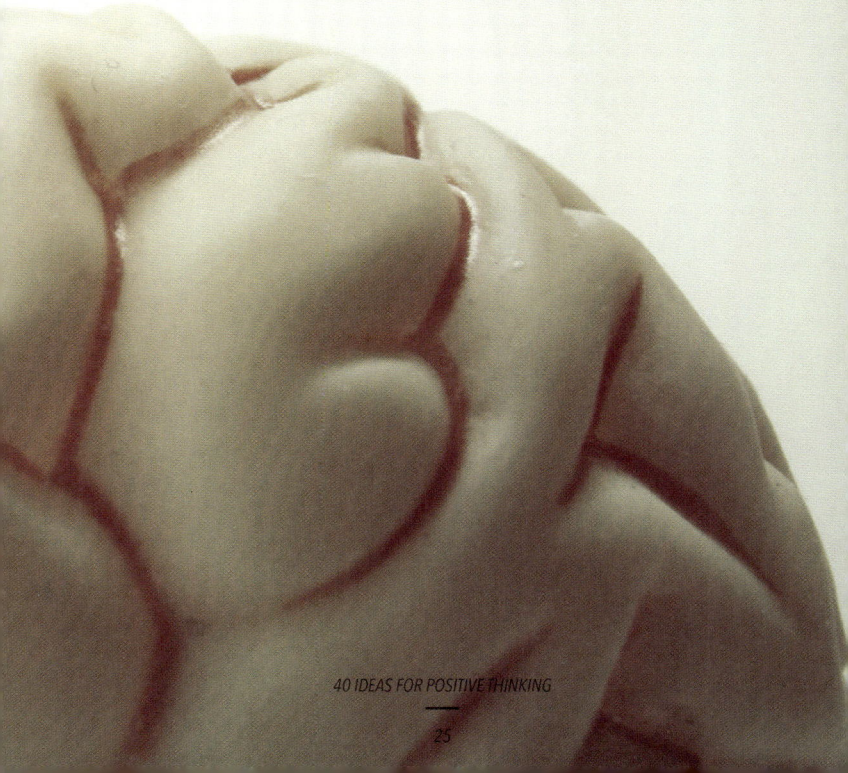

04

Target...What You Want

If one is hungry and walks into a supermarket,
the likely outcome is that one will buy
too much food.

In a place where tempting products are available,
like a supermarket, you can be sure
you'll buy what you need
plus a whole lot more that you don't.

However, if you make a list of what you need,

you will tend to buy only what is on that list.

We need to know how to list the necessary things
we need to do in daily life. The first things on our
list are the most important,
those things with the most responsibility
or obligation attached to them.

If every morning we haven't set targets for ourselves like
the work tasks we need to accomplish,
the book we are going to finish reading,
we will find many things interfere and distract us
so that at the end of the day
we realize we haven't achieved anything concrete.

Therefore, it is important to set realistic small
goals for each day and to complete
them as planned.

Sometimes we intended to do something
and we can't complete it
because life has a funny way of throwing up
unplanned issues. In such cases, don't worry,
just try again tomorrow.

40 IDEAS FOR POSITIVE THINKING

If we have a clear target, we will not get lost.

· ·

Write down your goals for each day,
in the morning before leaving home,
and try to achieve them.

(HAVING SENSIBLE TARGETS ALSO HELPS YOU
TO AVOID NEGATIVE THINKING
AND BAD INFLUENCES, RIGHT?)

05

Have Breakfast... Everyday

Young children aged 1-3 years require 1,200 kilocalories of energy per day
Young children aged 4-6 years require 1,450 kilocalories of energy per day
Young children aged 7-9 years require 1,600 kilocalories of energy per day

Boys aged 10-12 years require 1,850 kilocalories of energy per day
Boys aged 13-15 years require 2,300 kilocalories of energy per day
Boys aged 16-19 years require 2,400 kilocalories of energy per day

Girls aged 10-12 years require 1,700 kilocalories of energy per day
Girls aged 13-15 years require 2,000 kilocalories of energy per day
Girls aged 16-19 years require 1,850 kilocalories of energy per day

One should always start the day with breakfast.
This is because our brain functions more efficiently
when it has had fuel-energy to feed it.

Almost all medical books recommend people have breakfast
because the human body needs fuel
to function properly, and the brain is no different.

Our body also needs time to recharge
and recover lost energy,
just like a battery.

The best ways to recharge
the body's energy levels are by:
firstly, sleeping at least 6-8 hours a night
secondly, eating nutritiously covering
the 5 food groups across 3 daily meals
thirdly, drinking plenty of water
fourthly, finding constructive ways
to exercise all five senses.

{ This is very easy and practical.
And remember,
a healthy life is a happy life. }

66

YOUR MEAL ALWAYS
SMILES AT YOU !!!

—

We have to study hard and work hard

to get on in life, and to do this our body

requires enough energy to function

at maximum efficiency.

This should include protein to

power the brain too.

99

06

Make Everyone Around You...Laugh

There are those with a knack for making their friends laugh.
It is another way to be charming and attract positive attention.

But those walking the streets who have an unusual mind, they tend to upset someone at least 3 times a day.

Making someone happy is considered a creative and mind-nourishing way to train the brain.
It is also a natural way of avoiding negative thoughts.

Spreading humor and joy makes for a happy environment and ultimately leads to more positivity in life.

The way you utilize your brain
to generate something creative
includes several ways that can make
your colleagues laugh.
Such positive creativeness.

= *win + win + win* situation

The first win is that you exercise your brain
by thinking of something new and exciting
to tell your friends or colleagues.
In and of itself, this thought process
is a great way to reduce stress.

The second win is that by thinking this way
you boost your relationship-making skills.
Those who make conversations fun tend
to attract more attention and encourage
more people to want to share their company.

The third win is that you are helping others
to be happy. Be it a family member, friend or
colleague, they will appreciate that you
have made their day just that little bit brighter.
Such pleasurable moments encourage a
'feel good factor' in both of you.

Precautions
when telling a joke

★ ★ ★ ★ ★ ★ ★ ★ ★ ★ ★ ★ ★ ★ ★ ★ ★ ★

01 Don't tell a joke when a waiter or waitress brings your food and drink because if he or she laughs, their saliva might fly out at a 45 degree angle and you don't want the waiter or waitress's saliva in your food, do you?

02 Don't tell jokes at inappropriate times, such as at a funeral. The joke could offend and turn out to be a sad story for you.

03 Don't tell a joke to a friend while in a lift with strangers because the strangers may also want to laugh but feel they are unable to express their feelings.

04 Don't tell a negative joke about either a wife or husband in public. Other listeners may misinterpret your intended meaning.

05 Don't tell a joke while in the toilet because when laughing you could make others miss their aim and make a mess of the place.

Instructions for telling a joke

★ ★ ★ ★ ★ ★ ★ ★ ★ ★ ★ ★ ★ ★ ★ ★ ★ ★

01 Put on a jovial expression when telling a joke. If you look too serious, your audience may not realize you are relating a funny story and could misconstrue your meaning.

02 Gossiping about your parents-in-law is allowed because you can't tell this story at home. If you don't share it with others, you might somehow feel frustrated.

03 You should first try out a joke on those people you know enjoy a good laugh. If you start with those who are not sensitive to a joke, you might lose your self confidence if you fail to make your audience laugh.

04 By all means tell a dirty joke to your male friends. However, if the listeners are of the opposite sex, especially if you are flirting with one of them, don't tell a dirty joke, period!

05 It is OK to laugh at your own jokes. After all, you found it funny enough to be worth retelling, right? And don't explain a joke after you have told it. (Just walk away and let your audience work it out for themselves).

It took 6 days for God
to create the world
trees, streams, mountains,
animals, sea creatures,
fruits, vegetables.

God
worked really hard for
6 days.
But he left the 7th day
for himself and us
to rest happily.

"

Therefore,
whenever you feel tired and exhausted,
dejected, disappointed or run down,

always remember that

███████

you should stop and rest for
at least one day a week
to relieve stress and
recharge your batteries.

"

Pay No Attention to Back-stabbing and Rumors

81% of bad stories are sure to spread while just 13% of good stories spread.

People tend to like to listen to others' bad news.
We also like to pass on negative news relating to others.

This is especially true among uneducated classes because it gives people a feeling of being better off than others.

Delighting in the misfortune of others allows us
an illusionary feeling of temporary happiness.
But in the long run such a way of thinking becomes a poisonous habit
and reflects badly on a person's character.

* * * * * * * * * * * * * * * * * *

There is a law of nature called
The Law of Attraction
and it is powerful.

* * * * * * * * * * * * * * * *

It basically says that our thoughts are a magnet,

so that if we think positively,
we will attract positive things in our lives.

* * * * * * * * * * * * * * * *

Conversely, if we think negatively,
we will attract bad things
or bad luck to our lives.

* * * * * * * * * * * * * * * *

Hence, don't gossip about others.
If you think of someone in such
a negative fashion,
misfortune could easily come to you too.

GOOD TIME
IS BED TIME

"

Don't be
a credulous person

especially when listening to issues
of a negative or controversial nature.

If someone tries to involve you
in scandalous talk of a slanderous nature,
simply say you're not interested
or

"pretend to fall asleep."

"

08

View The World...
As It Should Be Viewed

If you want to teach your child to swim,
don't be afraid that he or she may swallow
a bit of water in the process.

If you want to teach your child to walk,
don't be afraid that he or she may fall a graze a knee.

If you want to teach your child to play football,
don't be afraid if your child is hit by the ball.

If you want your child to go to school,
don't be afraid he or she may fight with classmates.

If you want to teach your child to be good at working,
don't be afraid he or she may overwork themselves occasionally.
This is what life is like.
Life is filled with ups and downs,
happiness, sorrow, loneliness and love.

Living life properly is all about striking a balance.
It is similar to composing
a picture filled with various colors, all of which
contribute to the beauty of the whole.

In creating a delicious dish,
we use a combination of various flavors,
sour, sweet, salty, spicy and so on.

The secret to success is getting the ingredients and
seasoning mixed to the perfect proportion.

If we learn to have a positive attitude towards
living life, we will have a happy, balanced viewpoint.

We may not be richer or better off than before
but our thoughts are in harmony
and that helps us to see a more beautiful world
from the same old position we have always occupied.

Neither the world nor life
has changed, but when
we see it from a different angle,
with a different attitude,
the world can be a more
beautiful place.

THE BEST MOMENT
**IS THE DAY THAT WE
GIVE SOMETHINGS**
SPECIAL TO THE ONE WE LOVE.

LIVING
LESSON

Life is always teaching us lessons.
Keep all good experiences
in a beautiful box
and revisit them when you miss them.

Throw away

all the bad memories.

09

Keep Smiling and Laughing

We have to try to smile in every situation.

This might be difficult for a skinny person because
from a young age it tended to be the tubby kids
that were most cheerful.

They laughed easily.
They ate and slept well and were happy all the time.
They were cute with their chubby cheeks.

Remember, one smile could prolong your life by 2 minutes
and one laugh could extend your life by another 5 minutes.

There is no disadvantage to smiling.
Rather such displays of happiness and laughter help to make
the world a better place day by day.

For some people **smiling** is a **hard thing** to do. It might be because of stress, which encourages his or her face to look strained.

Some people lose their looks early because they wear a permanent frown.

Scientists haven't yet discovered why some peoples' looks deteriorate faster than others.

After God
created this world,
He creates a round
red ball
and called that ball
"happi-
ness"

At first God hid the ball of happiness in a **mountain.** But humans eventually found this "happiness".

Then God hid the ball of happiness **in the sea,** but again humans found it.

Finally, God hid the ball of happiness **in the heart of humans,** and from then on millions of humans haven't be able to find **happiness.**

(There has been someone relating this story for a long time but there is no evidence as to where the story actually originated from.
However, let me, the author, use this example here to help you find happiness in life easier. Thank you.)

A CHILD NEVER NEEDS A LESSON
ON HOW TO SMILE
BUT MANY ADULTS NEED ONE.

"

Smile

Smile everyday.

Children smile

and laugh easily,

but

after they have grown up

why it is so hard for them to smile

???

"

10

Hug + Love + Touch

Westerners greet one another by touching.

They shake hands, hug, kiss each other on the cheek
and kiss the back of a lady's hand.
These are customs and traditions that promote
physical connectivity.

Because touching can be
perceived through the skin's nerves,
one of the five senses remember.
The information from touching
is sent to the brain and the experienced stored away.

One of the reasons for **touching** is to receive warmth from the opposite party.

{ Sometimes, **touch** means much more than words. Sometimes a **hug** can convey something more than is expected. }

That is a feeling of **warmth** and **togetherness**, the banishing of **loneliness**. So how do we get **close to** someone?

In some families, the members hardly touch each other at all.
The mother and father never hug their children.

And many children grow up without experiencing such closeness.
Does that impact them in later life?

The warmth from touching certainly creates closer relationships.

In families where physical closeness is the norm, children dare to speak more openly to their parents.

They feel closer and become more accepting.

When children become friends with their parents,
their need to find additional warmth
from outside the family is lessened.
They are more open to discussing
their feelings with parents.
When they have a problem, they know
they can consult a loving parent for advice.

In fact,

it isn't only children who need this warmth.
Adults also benefit from such closeness too.

We can start this process of bonding

by hugging our children every morning
before leaving home
and every evening
when we return from work.

Hug each other everyday

and remember that
you are never too old for a hug.
Such warmth should exist
from generation to generation within a family.

HUGGING YOUR BABY IS FREE OF CHARGE.

HUGGING YOUR MOM IS FREE OF CHARGE.

HUGGING YOUR PARENTS IS AVAILABLE
AND NO PAYMENTS ARE NEEDED.

MOST OTHER WAYS OF FINDING HAPPINESS
ARE SURE TO COST MUCH MORE.

Tell your loved ones that you love them.
Hold their hands and give them frequent hugs.
Fail to do so and you will become an empty shell.

★ ★ ★ ★ ★ ★ ★ ★ ★ ★ ★ ★ ★ ★ ★ ★ ★ ★ ★

It costs nothing to give someone a hug!

"

Show your love...
and express
your feelings.

"

To love...
but not express your feelings
is a missed opportunity
you may live to regret.

11

Don't Be Too Serious

What is the best way to catch a thieving monkey?

1). Place a lasso trap baited with food on the floor for the monkey to step into. When he does, pull the rope and trap him.

2). Use a shotgun to shoot the monkey or scare him off by firing into the sky.

3). Use a steel cage and leave the door open, seducing the monkey in with tempting food. When the monkey steps in to pick up food, the trap will close.

In reality, all three methods are wrong. They might be effective in catching the monkey but in the end but they are not the best way.

In the 1st example the monkey might be too fast and get away with free food.

In the 2nd example using a shotgun might be too cruel. It is not trapping but hunting and in any case, the noise from the gun might frighten the monkey away but it can always come back.

The 3rd example can only be effective once because the monkey is very smart. If one of their monkey friends is trapped, the rest of the monkeys relay an alert message to their companions to be wary and they will never return.

The experienced animal expert will tell you that

1). If you want to catch a monkey, you need to understand the monkey's behavior.

2). The door to the problem will only open with the right key.

3). If you want to solve the problem, you need to be smarter than the monkey.

The easiest way to catch a thieving monkey is to

1). Use a narrow-necked brass vase or jar with a small opening in it.

2). Put a banana in the vase or jar.

3). Put the trap where the monkeys do their stealing.

When the monkey tries to steal the banana, it will run away grasping the stolen object tightly. The brass jar will not break but it is heavy and that slows the monkey down. However,
because a monkey is a monkey and won't give up its food easily, it won't let go of the banana. Thus, it becomes a slow thieving monkey that can't climb a tree, making it easy to catch.

If we are smarter than the problem, we can solve it easily.

We have to learn to **let go sometimes.**
When burdened with a **serious problem** we sometimes

slow ourselves down
by carrying it about with us everywhere.

Just like the monkey keeps a tight hold on its
favorite food, we are **trapped by life.**

Thus the trap of money
keeps us struggling because we want more.
We fail to think of what is **"sufficient"**, of what is **"enough"**.

Equally, the trap of fame and celebrity
keeps us partying every night just in case the paparazzi
are out and about, because we don't want to miss the
opportunity of getting our picture in the hi-so pages
of magazines with all the other beautiful people, do we?

The trap of chasing profit
makes many people sleepless and causes them to ignore
the fundamentally important things in life, such as family and friends.

The trap of success makes
many people want to follow
successful people. And yet the followers
have no idea of how to engineer their own success.

40 IDEAS FOR POSITIVE THINKING

★ ★ ★ ★ ★ ★ ★ ★ ★ ★ ★ ★ ★ ★ ★ ★ ★ ★ ★

If we behave like the thieving **monkey,**
grasping at everything and refusing to let go,
we will be trapped easily.

If we **let go** of what is not ours
and live a normal life within our means, we will be happy.

We get nothing for free in this world.
The temptations are many,
not just **bananas** but **gold**, **shares**, **fame**, etc.

The banana is used to attract **monkeys** to the trap
Gold is used to attract the **materialistic** to the trap
Shares are used to attract the **greedy** to the trap
Fame is used to attract the **wannabes** to the trap

If you want to be **free** of many problems,
just **let go**. Don't be like the monkey grasping the brass jar
while trying to run away.

And rest assured, others will know
you are being trapped!!

DON'T
BE TOO
SERIOUS !!!

"

Don't cram heavy problems into your brain,

because the brain can only cope with so much.

Give it too much to process and, like a computer,

it can freeze.

Try to make your body and mind happy.

Try to make your outlook 10 years younger than your actual age.

But don't try to act like a youngster in order to flirt

with younger people,

you don't want to be perceived a "dirty old man!"

"

12

Love...Love...Love

You don't have to be a beauty queen
to love children and animals.
To love makes us happy.

Love wild animals

Love plants

Love cats

Love colleagues

Love the environment

Love your world

Love reading

Love schoolmates

Love strangers

Love your enemy

Love that is not recommended

is

loving a roommate who is the same sex,
loving a schoolmate who already has a girlfriend or boyfriend,
loving a colleague who is already married,

stealing something from someone
stealing another person's pet

loving an old man (who is a dirty old man!!).

"

A LOVE STORY
IS ALWAYS A CLASSIC

"

13

Don't Compare With Others

All lives are valuable.
Everyone has his or her own path to walk.

Therefore, don't worry about who…
might be better or worse than us.

Don't waste your time thinking about who…
might be richer or poorer than you.

Don't worry about whose father
might be better connected
or which family is more prestigious

because comparing life in this way
can only lead to feelings of negativity.

Of course,
are those who look at life from another,
equally negative perspective.

They compare their lives with those
who are lower down the social pecking
order, so as to feel
more advantaged; 'happier'.

However, when such folk meet those who are richer or smarter,
they can't help but compare themselves with the new comers.

And such comparisons end up
making them feel inadequate

and unhappy!

WHY DO SOME
PEOPLE LIKE
TO COMPARE
THEMSELVES
WITH OTHERS
???

"

We all have our good points.

Just look at the good things
about your friends
and you will be happy.

"

14

Take...Good Care...Of Your Heart

If our heart beats 60 times per minute
In one hour, our heart beats 3,600 times
In one day, our heat beats 86,400 times
In one month, our heart beats 2,592,000 times
In one year, our heart beats 31,536,000 times

By the time we are 30 years old,
our heart has already beaten 946,080,000 times

If we live until 80 years of age,
our heart will have beaten 2,522,880,000 times

Hence, you must take care of your heart.
Those who find it hard to love could have hearts as hard as stone.
Conversely, those who love too liberally run the risk
of having their heart hurt often.
Try to be a "sensitive-hearted person".

There are two worlds,
the external world
and the internal world.

The external world
is
the world we see when we open our eyes and look around.
It is a brash world full of distractions
and the temptation of alluring things.
It often keeps us away from who we really are.

The internal world
is
the world within our own minds.
It is the world we see from our mind's eye,
the world we see when we close our eyes,
the peaceful world which allows us to look into
our own heart.

The same heart that has been beating all our life.
The same heart that makes us strong.
The same heart that has never given up no matter
how many obstacles we face.

Make sure you say thank you to your heart!!!
It has kept you happy and going strong up to the present.

LOVE
YOU

PUT YOUR HEART INTO A BOX
TAKE CARE OF YOUR HEART

The heart's size is equal to that of a fist.

It is located slightly to the left of center in the chest. Use it well.

Use it

to love your family more, to love your friends more, to love your own self too.

15

Easy Challenge and **Fun Life**

We often feel we are being challenged,
and sometimes we face
very difficult challenges in life.
Challenges seemingly too difficult for one's heart to handle,

and yet we prevail.
We struggle on and we learn life's lessons.

Our lives are a series of stories that we pass on
to following generations in the hope that our experiences
will help them through their difficult challenges.

What made us stronger yesterday makes them
strong today.

Life's lessons apply to everyone.

They teach us what is
right and wrong.

They teach us to carry on
and not to be disheartened.

If we can take all the positives in this life experience
and apply them to a better way of living,
we have reached
the true meaning of the term

"positive thinking"

WE CAN ADJUST TIME

BUT WE CAN NEVER GET IT BACK.

WE CANNOT CHANGE SOMETHING IN THE PAST BUT WE CAN CHANGE OUR FUTURE.

16

PASSED AND PAST

There was a young doctor who was 35 years of age.
One day he examined his mother
and found something wrong with her stomach.

He urged the hospital's surgery team
to immediately operate on his mother.
The team discovered that the doctor's mother
had a strange, hard object in her womb.

After being thoroughly examined,
they came to the conclusion that the hard object
was the remains of a child's body
who the surgeons said was the same age as the doctor.

The fact was that the object in
his mother's stomach was his twin
but they had not been born together.

Later that evening,

the young doctor was standing watching the sun set.

The young doctor was thinking that

he was such a lucky person
being born and being able to see this world.

He was not left in this mother's womb.

He realized that
He was lucky to breathe.
He was lucky to see the bright sky.
He was lucky to see the sky at night.
He was lucky to see the rain, thunderstorm and lightning.
He was luck that he could wander around.
He was lucky to have a lot of friends.

He was lucky to laugh when happy.
He was lucky to enjoy life with his schoolmates.
He was lucky to talk with his colleagues.
He was lucky to have the job he always wanted.
He was lucky to be able to hug his father and mother.
He was lucky to have met his girlfriend.
And he thought that…

he was lucky to have his life, until now.

IN TIME
ON TIME
SHOW TIME
REGULAR TIME
PRIME TIME
GOOD TIME
BAD TIME
RIGHT TIME

Let's think about

if we compete for happiness,
will we get a lot of benefits in life?

Those who **value the importance of time**
will not let time fly without
doing anything.

He or she will spend all their
precious time
making his or her life

"

Happy,
Peaceful
and Relaxed.

"

17

EARTH AND BEAUTY

Our Earth has more than one view we can look at.
The world can be seen as being cruel.
The world can be seen as being beautiful.

The world can be seen as full of happiness.
The world can be seen as full of suffering.
The world can be viewed as greedy and lustful.

From some views, the world is a place full of challenges,
a world that some have surrendered without
any attempt to fight.
The world will always be full of fighting no matter
if anyone uses all their energy to stop it.
The world for some people is boring and sad.

The world can be seen as being full of people we pay respect to.
The world from some people's view
is full of deceitful people and chaos.

Life has only
one choice.
You can choose
which view point you
want to see
because the world
is always the same
every day.

No matter where

or when we were born,

we can be

happy...

can't we

???

HUMANS AND **CHICKENS**

ARE ALWAYS HAPPY

WHEN THEY ARE WITH THEIR FAMILY.

18

RIGHT AND **HAPPY**

A new couple were on their honeymoon
a couple of weeks after getting married.

They decided to go to the beach.
As they walked along the beach hand in hand,
all of a sudden, they heard the sound of an animal:
"oink, oink, oink, oink".

The wife said to her husband
"that dog is crying so loudly".

The husband thought for a minute and said,
"I think that's the sound of a pig".

Then the noise stopped.

They continued their walk when

they heard the cry of the animal for a second time:
"oink, oink, oink, oink".

The wife said to her husband
"that dog is crying very loudly, don't you think so?"

The husband knew it wasn't the sound of a dog.
"It's the sound of a pig I'm sure…It's not a dog".

Suddenly,

They heard the sound of the animal a third time:
"oink, oink, oink, oink".

The wife said to her husband
"That dog might need something, that's why
it keeps crying so loud.
Don't you think so?"

The husband was sure it wasn't the sound of a dog.
"Really, it is not the sound of a dog.
It's a pig I'm absolutely sure of it."

The couple continued along the beach when they heard the sound of the animal for the fourth time:

"oink, oink, oink, oink".

The wife turned to her husband
with tears in her eyes and asked,
"That dog is over there and is crying loudly.
Don't you think so?"

The husband looked at his beloved wife
who had tears rolling down her face.
He didn't want his wife to be sad, so he said,

"Yes, sweetheart..

I think that dog is crying really loudly."

What is important to our life?

The points of view of all people are different

because people have a brain, thoughts and different views.

Many people might not know
"What were they born for?"
"Why were they born?"

These two questions do not depend on

who asks the question

but it depends on who answers
the question and who they are.

Some might answer

"He was born to be a judge"

He has to tell everyone the truth

because the truth is the truth.

There have been many cases where a father

and his child are fighting

because the father thinks that black is better than white

while his child thinks that white is better than black.

Since the father has more authority,
he forces his son to leave home.

Are we born for a particular reason or
does our life depend on
the truth or being right?

The difference between a pig and a dog
The difference between white and black
The difference between a duck and a hen
The difference between left and right

Are we born to triumph over those we love?
We sometimes forget that when we are sad,
who stands beside us.

When we are sick and admitted to hospital,
how many people will come and look after us
and be with us 24 hours a day?

Those are the people in our family;
our father, mother, brother, sister, children
and grandchildren.
No other people from outside our family
will be with us throughout our life.

We might forget that
the word "happiness" exists in this world.

Happiness is another path
that we can always choose to follow.

★ ★ ★ ★ ★ ★ ★ ★ ★ ★ ★ ★ ★ ★ ★ ★ ★

No one puts up a barrier
to prevent you
from experiencing happiness.

★ ★ ★ ★ ★ ★ ★ ★ ★ ★ ★ ★ ★ ★ ★ ★ ★

It is only youwho does not know
where your happiness is.
You don't know what to do.

Try to look for it from now on
and see where your happiness is.

Spend your life with it
and you will know
how happy your life is.

You don't have to worry
whether it is a pig or a dog.

Just go to sleep!!!

You don't need to know why...

people always fight???

**A DOG NEVER
CARES WHAT
A HUMAN IS
THINKING.**

**A DOG HAS ITS
OWN LIFE AND
ENJOYS IT
IN DOG STLYE.**

Knowing how to build a family that is
as happy as being in paradise
does not depend on anything,
or anyone,
it is only ourselves.

- -

**We sometimes have a lot of conditions
and reasons for doing something
for ourselves.**

- - - - - - - - - - - - - -

Is it possible to find only one reason
in order for us to do something
for the ones we love
and those who love us?

- -

Try to make them happy
because we don't have to wait for happiness
as it is already right here in our heart.

{ When you have found
your heart,
you will be **happy.** }

19

··

WATCH AND LISTEN

··

We choose to consume things.

Things that happen in our life
are recorded in our brain.
Likewise, there are a lot of films we can choose,

it just depends on us to make that choice.
If we want to be happy,

we will choose to watch happy movies,
or a romantic comedy that makes us smile and laugh.

Is that the way to make us happy?

Some knowledgeable adults have noted
that if people watch violent movies,
they tend to have violent behavior.
It might not be true.

★ ★ ★ ★ ★ ★ ★ ★ ★ ★ ★ ★ ★ ★ ★ ★ ★

We are conscious beings,
and we can warn our self to think twice
before we do something bad.

★ ★ ★ ★ ★ ★ ★ ★ ★ ★ ★ ★ ★ ★ ★ ★ ★

However, when we lose our consciousness,
we move to something that's called
the "sub-consciousness".

It might unintentionally reveal something cruel

We can choose what we want to be
We can choose what we want to do
We can choose what we want to watch
as well !!!

LOOK AT
GOOD
THINGS

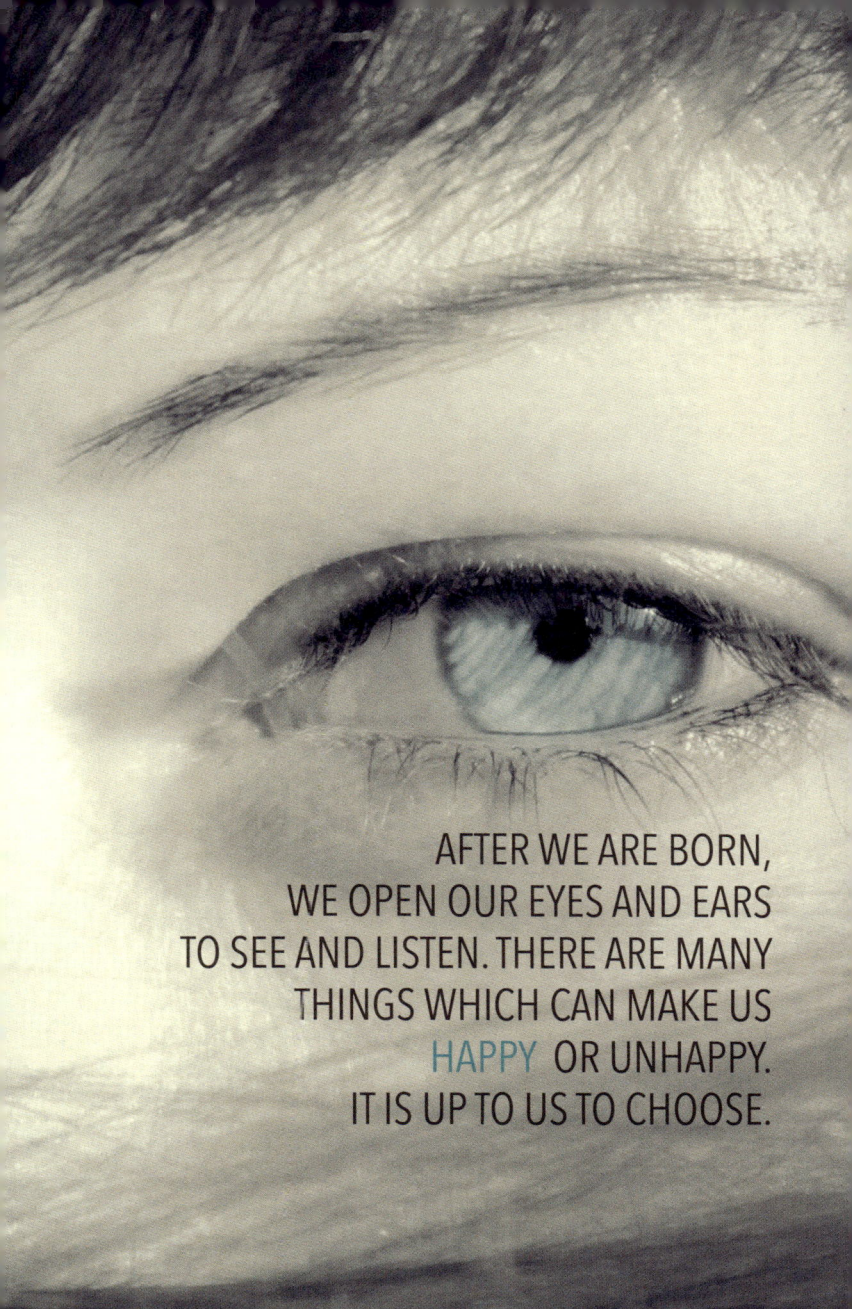

AFTER WE ARE BORN,
WE OPEN OUR EYES AND EARS
TO SEE AND LISTEN. THERE ARE MANY
THINGS WHICH CAN MAKE US
HAPPY OR UNHAPPY.
IT IS UP TO US TO CHOOSE.

20

....

READ AND READ

....

There are people who are called "scholars"
or
"knowledgeable people".

There are many of these
educated people in the world.

All these scholars have one thing
in common which is they tend to
"read a great deal of books".

The majority of the people in the world know more about
who lost their job, who went to jail,
who made who pregnant,
who dumped who and so on.

They know everything apart from themselves.

They don't know how to better their life.
They don't know how to make themselves successful.

There are far more people that are not considered
"scholars"
but they are successful in their career,
and family life.
These people are generally book-loving people.

Good books are created by the best thoughts, **not by the best printing machine.**

21

FAMILY AND **ACTIVITY**

Without a family,
how can we live happily?

If we don't have anyone beside us,
just turn around,
and we will see our family is always beside us.

Whenever we are very tired,
there are not many people we can lean on.

Real happiness
or permanent happiness for someone
is probably
to live in a happy family.

There are

3

rules

to make a happy family
that should be followed by the family leader
and everyone in the family.

The first rule

The family leader should provide good things
to make a happy family.

The second rule

Family members should provide good things
to make a happy family.

The third rule

Everyone in the family should provide good things
to make a happy family.

If all family members can follow
these three rules,
Then you have a happy family

"
FAMILY
=
HAPPINESS
"

22

**There are 2 English homonymic words
that have the same spelling;**
Present which means the current period of time
and present, which means a gift.
These two homonyms are similar to
one of the teachings in Buddhism which says,
"Do our best for the present day".
and
"be mindful of the present moment".

All these tell us
to live the "happiest" life at "present"

because the "present" moment is the gift that everyone has.
However, "not everyone can achieve happiness
from the present moment."

PRESENT

=

PRESENT

=

PRESENT

40 IDEAS FOR POSITIVE THINKING

PRESENT

PAST

FUTURE

Do your best today
and

see good things
happen tomorrow.

23

GOOD AND RESPECT

An old warrior
walks up a hill every morning
to pay his respect to his mentor's grave.

He takes with him a sword to perform
a veneration ritual to his mentor.
He has done this everyday
since his mentor passed away.

He does it willingly
because his mentor taught him how to use a sword.

For years, he has done the same thing
because he has an inner passion
to do everything from the heart.

Many people forget to be grateful to
the ones who offered them kindness.
They forget the kindness from
their parents and their friends.

The great warrior

is not a person who can win every battle

But the greatest warrior
is
a person with gratitude
who repays the kindness
and never betrays anyone.

There are many people who succeed in their career by betrayal and backstabbing.

Unless God wants it that way,
traitors will never be successful.

24

**If we plan a journey
we will know our final destination
and the right directions to take us there.**

It would be hard to reach a destination
if we started a journey without a plan.

There are plenty of stories that happen in life,
but we usually forget that
some of what has happened are important to our life,
as we overlook them and pay attention
to something that's more tempting.

There might be something we see as
"The Golden Opportunity" in life,
but actually, it might possibly be a Trap of Life.

Many undergraduates who enroll
at university don't like what they are studying.
They know neither which subjects they want to
study nor do they have the desire to learn.
They simply study according to what their parents want,
to follow friends, or follow someone's advice.
It is certain that these undergraduates have no idea
what they want to achieve.

These people's lives are just like

someone who catches the next train
but has no idea where to go or where to get off.

In front of us is a wild river

If we jump in and let the water take us
how long can we stand the pounding of the water?
When we have no idea where we are going
we let go of our body and follow the current.
But what if at the end there is a dangerous waterfall?

The result is the same as if we spend our life aimlessly,

walking on a dark street with poor visibility.
It is possible we might fall down a hole or walk into a pole
or we could be accidentally injured.

The light at the end of a tunnel

is the only thing that enables us to see in the pitch black

and provides us with the only way to escape

from an unfamiliar place of darkness.

Just even a little amount of illuminating light
has the same value as the North Star that guides
jungle trekkers, explorers and the adventurous
to walk in the right direction in the darkness of night.

**Most aimless people don't know the right direction
and so they don't know if the way they are walking
will lead them to success, a maze or a vast field.**

It is like they are being forced on to a train
following their friends to make it on time
before the train departs.

**In the end, there are a lot of people on the train,
and all have no idea where the train will take them.**

**People who have no passion in life,
no idea what they should learn,
or which job they should do,
are so pitiful and unfortunate.**

Stop to think about your goal.
When you have figured it out
You will see a light at the end of the tunnel
just like the North Star
Something you have been searching for your whole life.

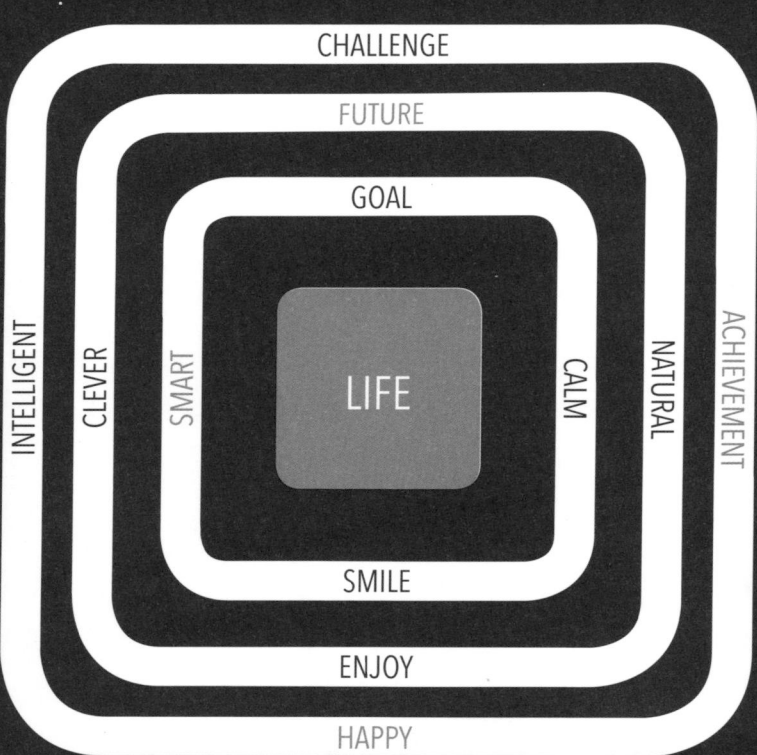

CHALLENGE

FUTURE

GOAL

INTELLIGENT CLEVER SMART LIFE CALM NATURAL ACHIEVEMENT

SMILE

ENJOY

HAPPY

40 IDEAS FOR POSITIVE THINKING

If you practiced writing down the **goals for your life**
since you were young, you will know what you really want,
and in which direction you should go to reach your
destination before starting your journey.

The goal for life
is not only financial security
but also achievements in education, your well being,
your career, familyand paying back to the community.

If you set your goal on **education,**
you have to study hard and do your best,
then, you can reach your goal.

If you set your goal on **happiness,**
you have to search for it... then,
you will find your **happiness.**

25

WORK AND GOAL

Once upon a time, there was a foolish donkey
who lived its life day to day, thinking of nothing.
It walked aimlessly into the forest.

While the foolish donkey was walking in the forest,
he met a monkey.
The donkey asked the monkey,

"Hey, what are you doing?"
"I'm collecting food for winter
which will come soon," answered the monkey.

"During winter, it snows heavily
and we can't go outside for several months."

The foolish donkey didn't care much about what he was hearing,
he just kept walking and walking in the forest.

Meanwhile, the monkey and his family were helping each other to collect food for the coming winter.

When winter came, it snowed heavily everyday.
All the animals in the forest
retreated to the shelters they had made
and where they had stored enough food to last for several months.

Only an outsider like the foolish donkey
didn't know how bad the winter could be
in this forest.

The poor donkey had neither shelter nor food,
while it snowed heavier and heavier everyday.
All the plants that the donkey could eat
had been covered with snow and were frozen solid.

Soon after that,
the foolish donkey died.

FIRE ON THE TARGET

BEFORE YOU ARE FIRED

For some people,

★ ★ ★ ★ ★ ★ ★ ★ ★ ★ ★ ★ ★ ★ ★ ★ ★ ★ ★

Work = Life
and
Life is to work

★ ★ ★ ★ ★ ★ ★ ★ ★ ★ ★ ★ ★ ★ ★ ★ ★ ★ ★

Living our life in a proper way can save our life.
To work without a principle, strategy and knowledge
is like to work basically by our "instinct".

Instinct keeps us alive,
but only when we live in a forest like wild animals.

As human beings, we have something greater than
"instinct"
and we call it "intellect"
This allows us to increase our knowledge and capabilities.

If we work by utilizing our strategy, knowledge,
professionalism, skills, joy and love,

we can survive in our highly competitive society
and live our life happily.

26

THINK AND HAPPY

**In 1 day, there are 1,440 minutes
Or 86,400 seconds**

Out of those 86,400 seconds remember
a happy moment for **10 seconds each day.**

Then in **1 year,** you will be "happy" for **3,650 seconds.**

In **10 years,** you will be "happy" for **36,500 seconds.**

By the time you reach **50,**
you will have been "happy" for **182,500 seconds**
and that is equal to **33 full-length movies,**
each with a duration of 1 and a half hours.

**If this is the way we all think,
won't we have more happiness in life?**

Life is not that hard if we think it's easy.
If we know which questions about life
we should ask ourselves,
if we know exactly what we want from our life,
if we know who we are living for, others or ourselves?

**If we know whether we should love
ourselves more or love others more.**

If we know how worthy our life is

For those
who are searching for "happiness"
you can find it any time, and any period of time.

★ ★ ★ ★ ★ Happiness ★ ★ ★ ★ ★
can be achieved during our entire life.

★ ★ ★ ★ ★ Happiness ★ ★ ★ ★ ★
happens when we wake in the morning,
when we breathe, see, hear,
sense and eat. Even when we smell pleasing scents.

★ ★ ★ ★ ★ Happiness ★ ★ ★ ★ ★
happens when someone takes care of us
and when we take care of someone.

Where is happiness?
What is happiness?

Everyone has a different answer to these questions
because happiness is an individual matter
based on personal preferences.

So,

{ just do whatever you love
and you will be happy. }

THE BEST DAY IS THE DAY

WE KNOW OUR DREAM

IF YOU DO NOT REMEMBER,
YOU SHOULD WRITE IT DOWN.

IN THE NEAR FUTURE,
IT MAY BE IMPORTANT TO YOU
AND FOR YOUR INSPIRATION.

27

Stay Healthy
HEALTH AND CARE

**Suppose we all have a twin,
and our twin is called "Mr. Health".**

Mr. Health is always with us everywhere we go.
We are the leader and our twin is the follower.
Whatever we do will affect him as a consequence.

If we eat healthy food, Mr. Health will be healthy.
If we exercise, Mr. Heath will be fit and firm.

If we drink alcohol, Mr. Health will get drunk and be unhealthy.
If we don't exercise, Mr. Health will become weaker.

*When Mr. Health becomes too sick,
he will die, and we will die with him
because we are twins
who are a reflection of each other.*

"

By the time we have realized that

good health is priceless,

it might be too late.

"

GOOD HEALTH
GOOD LIFE
GOOD BODY

In the past, a lot of people made a lot of money

but they forgot to keep themselves healthy.

All the money they made was paid to doctors

and spent taking care of their health in hospital.

So why bother making a lot of money and

then forget to take care of your health?

28

FORGIVE AND FORGET

**Anger is stupidity
Furiousness is insanity**

Furiousness and hatred
takes us away from

"positive thinking"

We have to teach ourselves
by practicing our mind to be endurable
by performing meditation, by having self-awareness
and to be mindful when doing any activities.

Unless we have self-awareness
we will lose control of our emotions
and will be easily affected by a bad temper.

If we learn to "forgive"
we will never be dragged into the loop of
stupidity and insanity.

CALM
CLEAR
COOL
CLEVER

Ordinary people

usually have these feelings;

Love, Greed, Anger, Lust

This is quite normal.

If we want to avoid one of these feelings,
then we should learn
how to cast off anger
and
start to forgive each other.

When you learn how to forgive,
you will live your life more happily
than ever.

29

. . . .

TIME AND VALUE

. . . .

Once we have set our goal,
we have the duty to reach it.

If anything tries to blocks us
from reaching our goal,

we should define it as **"nonsense"**.

Or if there is something not beneficial to us in any way,
we should also call that "nonsense".

Nonsense wastes our time,
messes with our minds
and even costs us money.

The reason some people become successful

faster than
other people
is because

they do not waste their time
on nonsensical matters.

"

TIME vs MONEY
WHAT IS MORE IMPORTANT ???

Do you know
how valuable time is
???

"

30

CHOOSE AND **LOVE**

Many people work in a career
they do not like
and it is not what they were born to do.

Many people didn't graduate in a subject they love
so they make excuses that they didn't study
what they should have done.

There are many excuses we can make
when we don't do what we love to do

**So, why don't we start doing
what we love now?**

Fortunately, some people know
which job they love,
and know what they want to be or to study.

Meanwhile, there are some people who don't know yet
what they love to do,
so, these people just aimlessly live their life day by day.

To discover for ourselves what we love

First,

look back to the past and think of
what really made you happy.

Second,

think of what you are doing now
if you are happy doing it or not.

Third,

try to figure out the future and
what we want to do in the next ten years.

That's the way to find out what you really love to do.
Make a review in your heart right now.

A lucky man

**has the chance to do
what he loves the most.
All of us can do
what we love as well.**

Just try it.

You can do it!

31

BEAUTY AND PRETTY

**When we dress smart,
we'll see a more beautiful world.**

When we see ourselves as being good looking,
our mindset will be better.

Our life will be even better.

In the past, we dressed up for others to see

but from now on, we should dress up for own ourselves,

because we all love to see beautiful things

that make us happy, don't we?

Everyone likes to look at beautiful things.

Therefore, dress up and first see yourself as being beautiful,

then reveal your beauty to others.

Those who can attract people from

their smart appearance

are usually **beautiful,**

from the inside out.

32

....

GOD AND FOOD

....

We do many things in life without thinking
how we might have an impact on others.

We eat food everyday but rarely think of the farmers.
We waste food and forget
how hard many farmers have worked to produce
the food on our table.

Before we eat an apple,
think of the people who picked and packed
the apples for us.

When we eat an omelette,
do we think of the chicken that laid the eggs for us?
When we drink a can of soda,
do we think of the sugar cane producers?

Under the capitalist society of today,
money has come to mean the value of life.
We use it to measure success
and how much each person can earn.

Therefore, a lot of people live their lives depending
on money which they have to work hard to earn.

There are a lot cf people who are greedy for
more money, precious stones and all kinds of assets.
They will happily backstab their colleagues
and betray their company
by leaking secret corporate information for a reward.

If we think of
everything we have consumed
from when we were babies until today,
we are sure to become grateful people.

{ A grateful person
is usually a good person
by nature. }

ENJOY YOUR FOOD

ENJOY YOUR LIFE

Thank God

for this meal

and

thank the person
who cooked it

as well.

33

SWEET AND ROMANTIC

People who live in warmer climates have
taste buds that are less sensitive to spicy food.
That's why people from tropical areas
usually eat spicier food than
people from cooler countries.

Those who live in a tropical climate
sometimes eat something sweet
like a dessert or fruit.

We should add a touch of sweetness to our life
and into our friends' lives as well.

To give something to someone,
it's not necessary to wait for a special occasion.

When we travel alone,
thinking of people we meet everyday ... is enough to be happy.

We can add sweetness

to our life,

———●———

by learning to do something romantic
for our loved ones,
so that life will be sweeter and better.

———●———

Our life has experienced
enough sour, salty, spicy
and bitterness.

———●———

It's time to

add a touch of sweetness
for a better life.

A DESSERT MAKES OUR LIFE
SO SWEET,
SO PLEASE TRY SOME.

MADE BY LOVE
MADE BY HEART

34

WALK AND **FRIEND**

There may be less than 5 people
we talk to each day.

We are their friend in need
and they are our friend in need as well.

If you love someone and care for them,
do something to let them know.

Don't just keep your feelings in your heart
tell them what you feel,
ask them how they are and let them know you care.
Don't you feel good doing this?

They will feel great,
and you will feel even greater.

If you love someone but never let them **know**
they will never be aware of
what you have done for them.
So, what benefit is this inaction to our life
???

HOLD MY HAND
HOLD YOUR HAND

Hold hands and walk together

whether you are a child or an adult.
It is always better to walk together than walk alone.

When walking alone, there will be no one to encourage you
if you feel down.
When walking alone, there will be no one to talk to
if you feel lonely.

{
When we are accompanied by
our friends,
our subordinates,
our bosses,
our parents and grandparents,
our spouse,
or our children;
}

although they might not be able to help us that much,
at least we have someone to talk to.

We don't need to live our life all alone
in this world.

35

GIVE AND TAKE

We talk to each other everyday
We assign them jobs everyday

They work for us everyday
They help us when we get tired
All of us are willing to help each other
although we are just colleagues.

If we think that all of our colleagues
share the same path of life with us,
We are friends forever,
and we should take care of each other.

Because if they get sick or are absent from work,
we will not be able to accomplish our job alone.

A boat	depends on	a river
A tiger	depends on	a jungle
A buyer	depends on	a seller
A boss	depends on	a subordinate
A pregnant lady	depends on	a midwife
A bully	depends on	a victim
A priest	depends on	a gospel
A washbasin	depends on	on water
A grandmother	depends on	a grandfather
A heavy item	depends on	a balance
A tree	depends on	soil
A crazy man	depends on	a psychiatrist
A knife	depends on	cutting board
A candidate	depends on	a vote
Everyone	depends on	each other

If in a year your subordinate
makes a coffee for you.

Pick 1 good day out 365 days
to make him or her a cup of coffee.

This will surprise them
and
you will be probably
be remembered and loved more.

(Just try it!!!)

36

CARD AND BIRTHDAY

When you receive a birthday card
from someone,
are you happy that
someone remembered your birthday?

Probably you are an important person in their life.
On the other hand,
when you a send a birthday card to a friend,
they will be happy
and possibly feel that
they are important to you.

They will feel good taking care of you
and this will make you feel great.

Such giving makes our life much better, doesn't it?

If all of us want to be
an important person to someone
then,
make them important to you first.

Because

anything we give,
we will be given back
with the same love
and feeling.

HAPPY **MONDAY** TO YOU
HAPPY **TUESDAY** TO YOU
HAPPY **WEDNESDAY** TO YOU
HAPPY **THURSDAY** TO YOU
HAPPY **FRIDAY** TO YOU
HAPPY **SATURDAY** TO YOU
HAPPY **SUNDAY** TO YOU

"Candles"

are so meaningful on a birthday cake.

"Kind words"

are so meaningful
to a person who is sad.

"Appreciation"

is so meaningful
to a person who has worked hard.

"Encouragement"

is so meaningful
to a person who feels down.

★ ★ ★ ★ ★ ★ ★ ★ ★ ★ ★ ★ ★ ★ ★ ★ ★ ★

When you want to say
something to someone,
make sure it is the right time.

★ ★ ★ ★ ★ ★ ★ ★ ★ ★ ★ ★ ★ ★ ★ ★ ★ ★

40 IDEAS FOR POSITIVE THINKING

37

START AND END

Many centuries ago, an old soldier
took his young son
to fight in a battle
against his country's enemy.

Unfortunately,
the old man who had killed a lot of enemies himself
saw his own son
being killed on the battlefield by an opponent.

The old man was overcome with grief
and burst into tears,
as he ran to his son's body

It took four men to carry him
off the battlefield.

After the battle had finished, the old soldier lived alone.

Everyone in the army felt so sad
for this soldier's great loss.
There was no celebration that night,
although they had won the battle.
It was a totally silent night
as everyone was overwhelmed with deep sorrow.

While everyone was grieving, the old soldier who had lost his beloved son was granted an audience with the king and said,

"Today is the saddest day of my life,
my sadness is not for the death of my son,
I am so sad because since he was born,
I never let him know how much I loved him."

(From the movie 300)

There are many ways to
share good feelings
with each other.

It could be an email, a card
or simply a few kind words.

Just do it before we become
heartless people.

38

NATURAL AND EFFECT

Some like to go to the "beach"
because they think that the sea is beautiful.

Some like to go to the "mountains"
because they think that mountains are beautiful.

Some like to go to a "waterfall"
because they think waterfalls are beautiful.

If we appreciate the beauty of nature
we will be rewarded by beautiful nature.

But more than that, being able to see
"beauty" in "ordinary things"
allows us to become more positive thinkers.

The most fortunate people

are not the richest people.

The fortunate are those who are happy

The fortunate are not happy because of the material things they can afford.

The fortunate can sleep easily without the need for sleeping pills and they wake up with a smile.

The fortunate are happy because they have full consciousness.

The fortunate can see happiness in the most ordinary things in everyday life.

They are happy to see the sunshine.
They are happy to breathe the morning's fresh air.
They are happy to hear the birds sing.
They are happy to enjoy a healthy breakfast.
They are happy to take a shower and dress well.
They are happy to be alive and able to make others happy too.

40 IDEAS FOR POSITIVE THINKING

IF YOU CAN SEE BEAUTY
IN A DROP WATER,
YOU WILL FIND MORE
HAPPINESS IN LIFE.

If you are able to see beauty
in all aspects of life,
you have a positive thought process.

Also,

when you think positively,

you can find happiness
more easily.

39

When you are stressed, it is likely that you are over-thinking a problem or issue.

Research reveals that
the best medicine for stress isn't found at the pharmacy
but can be found in exercise.

Exercise
is not limited by age or sex.
You can do whatever you feel up to physically.

Some might like to play basketball.
Some might like to play football, or judo, or karate,
or practice yoga,or try fencing, or skipping.

Heck, you might even enjoy
carrying your wife around the house!
Whatever you find suitable based on age
and personal preference.

As a result of exercise,
you will have...

01 Better blood flow

02 A better heart rate

03 Increased "adrenaline", a natural chemical that makes you happy (and costs no money)

04 A better body shape

05 Lower cholesterol

06 More energy

07 Healthier looks

08 Greater immunity

09 More efficient lung function

10 And new healthy friends to hang out with

HIDE AND SEEK

is a popular game among two groups of people.

The first group is kids aged 5-10
and
The second group is married men
who are oh so happy
when they can get out without their wives
being able to find them.

For kids playing hide and seek,
the last one to be found starts the next game as the seeker.
In this way everyone has fun.

However
for those guys who hide from their wives,
when they get found out
they don't get any chance to start over.

Tragically, the game ends
and no one has any fun.

40

DO **AND** LOVE TO DO

Love is what keeps us alive.

Just as water keeps a tree alive.
If a tree doesn't have water, it will die.

We humans can live without food for around 7 days
before we die.
But without water, we cannot last longer than 3 days.

Love encourages us
to live our lives in harmony.

Whenever we feel lonely,
when we are away from our loved ones,
we only have to picture their faces
and we smile.

Just thinking of them makes us happy.

Love

happens not only between people.

Love

also flourishes between people and their pets and
connections occur between the most unlikely
of partners.

Love

might happen between;
A man and a fish
A man and a worm
A man and a parasite
A spoon and a fork
A car and a steering wheel
A bear and a salmon

Some folk might even fall in love
with their own belly,
because they bring it with them
everywhere and at all times.

This is what we call...

A small "Circle" of love.

We can choose
our own way to live life.

But whichever path you choose,
walk it with love

and be happy with your choice.

{ Love what you do
and
do what you love. }

YOU CAN WALK ON
YOUR WAY

"

If you
love your job,
keep working

because
to be in a job you love
is so very rare.
It's like finding an outfit
in your favorite style
that fits perfectly.

"

Do what you love

We have many excuses
for our actions.
Excuses we use
to justify our choices.
Try doing something
without any excuse for once.
Do the thing you love
and you might achieve

something that you
didn't think was possible.

Love what you do

We also have many excuses

for why we don't love

whatever we're doing.

Of course there can be

millions of reasons

but when you love what you do,

all problems seem to

vanish.

It all depends on your mindset

and your heart.

Positive thinking

will open a new window to your heart.
Just as every coin has two sides,
so we must see both sides of life
– the positive and negative –
to understand how to live better.

Positive thinking

will teach you that "whatever happened,
it's all good".
Even those things that cause us to suffer provide lessons
that ultimately make us stronger.

To have positive thinking

you don't have to be rich
you don't have to be a graduate
you don't have to have a job
you don't have to own a car
you don't have to be married and have children.

We can learn how to think positively
at any time, irrespective of status and without
a worry as to the amount of cash in our wallets.
Everyone can think positively. There is nothing stop-
ping you from this moment on.

40 IDEAS FOR POSITIVE THINKING

Happiness

also can be achieved without any agenda,
with no concern for status,
and with no reason to prevaricate.

Happiness

is a simple state of being that is available to all
and achievable by all.

The angry person won't be happy
The happy person won't get angry

Whenever we feel a loss of control, whenever we
experience a bout of bad temper, whenever we resort to

bad or cruel language, or feel jealousy
or disappointment,
we chip away at our own happiness.

Those who love to gossip, judge others,
show hatredtowards others,
this kind of behavior may give a negative
feeling of temporary happiness.
But the reality is that this kind of person
is merely covering up latent feelings
of inferiority by picking on the weak points of others.

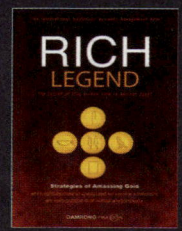

Rich Legend

Rich Legend shows you how to invest right and how to save your money the right way - income, costs, payments and also benefits: what is really important? A strategy on how millionaires and billionaires have done business since the ancient Egyptians, this is actually a manuscript for modern day businessman along with the RICH LEGEND that you can actually apply to your life.

Dream Come True

This book is suitable for two kinds of people: those people who have a dream and those people who have no dream. We can choose to live life believing in everything and waiting for our gods to bring us success or we can choose to pursue our dream and make it come true with our own two hands.

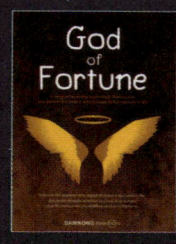

God of Fortune

This book features the secret of successful working. Businessmen, traders and workers who want to know how to overcome any difficult obstacles must read it. We all can bring success to our work only when we are blessed with virtue and braveness. Seven Secrets of the Legend of Success, there is only one person in a million who can find the God of Fortune.

Seven Angels

Seven Angels provides seven practical principles for those who want to be a "Good Leader". The Seven Angels can reveal to all of us useful leadership tips that will make you a smart leader: Top secrets for being both a happy and successful leader. Seven Angels who appeared in Rome to teach a young man who desired to be a "Great Leader" just like his father.

Marketing Idea

Marketing Idea is a book with lots of marketing ideas because marketing strategies are very different. It all depends on the products and the timing of the product launch. This book will give you the full walk through on every marketing circumstance that might occur.

Strategy + Idea

This book presents special hints on how to make your business strategy more effective. It reveals the business strategies of market leaders plus the strategies of the underdogs who want to be leaders but without investing too much capital. They still get great results to ensure the security of their business.

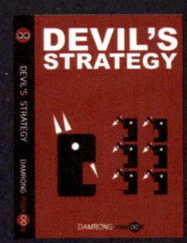

Devil's Strategy

f we are smaller than our competitor we need some backup to make us look stronger. Only great ideas and supreme talent will obtain the best results. Strategy is not only about WINNING, it's about TAKING IT ALL. A strategic talent can analyze a situation in every detail and use a strategy or plan to get the desired result.

Creative Management

This book tells you how to manage everything in your life. To have real happiness in life and to become successful. Smart people choose to manage, the wise ones choose to teach those who work for them, while the wiser than the wise deeply understand management theory and can get it to work in real life.

CEO Know + How

This book offers executives and CEOs' lessons in theoretical learning before they actually put plans into action. Executives need to use their knowledge correctly to grow and evolve their companies. Without knowing how to use their knowledge the right way, their company won't go anywhere. This book gives the directions to follow to make your company a success.

MARKETING Know + How

This book deals with the tricks and tips today's marketers need to know. The book gives clear information about marketing and is very easy to understand. If a marketer wants to do marketing without really understanding it, the target customers won't get the idea what the marketer wants to communicate and the product won't sell.

Management Know + How

This book provides tricks and tips about management that today's executives need to know for effective management. If an executive knew management theories clearly, all problems will be solved. Good personnel and a good working system affect the results. So, if an executive uses all the tricks and tips provided in this book to improve personnel and working system, his results will be better.

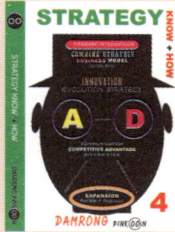

Strategy Know + How

This book provides strategies which are used in businesses. Approach strategies and defence strategies will be effective only if a businessmen can analyze the situatuation correctly. Problems occur when businessmen do not know how to use strategies at the right time. To attack an opponent without strategies will only bring a negative impacts to us and not our opponent. Businessmen need to know how and when to use a strategy.

I am Latte, You are Cappuccino

This is a book about humans, a manual for us to learn
how to understand humans, understand yourself
and understand others. We can compare a man's life to
a cup of coffee with different ingredients. For a cup of coffee
to be delicious and to feel right, it has been through lots of
processes to become the right coffee. The recipe to this
right coffee could change the lives of millions of people.

A Beautiful World is not enough

When two people look at the world, they see
it differently even though they both live in the
same world. This book shows how everything has
its own 'reason', why we are all 'destined' to be who
we are and why things happens the way they do.

The Best Leader

Good managers are different from excellent managers just as unproductive
managers are different from successful managers. This book outlines a variety
of managerial trains of thought for all types of executive. In the same position -
and coping with an identical situation - each type of manager would handle the
problems they face in a different manner. This book contains many real-world
scenarios for managers who need to make executive decisions; either in a smart
or foolish way.

Leader Secret

This book will open the door for those who need to improve their thoughts and
approach to leadership. Almost all excellent leaders have lacked virtue and morality
at one time or another. A good leader does not always need to be an excellent
role model. Learn to harness positive thinking to emphasize basic goodness and
responsibility in management. In businesses, it is possible to be successful without
taking advantage of others and this book provides a number of good ideas that
leaders can follow to improve their principles in the workplace, which in turn
benefits everyone in society.

Happiness Through Your Eye

Although we live in the same world, we are only able to see the world through our eyes. Sometimes, what "we see in our eyes" is far different from what us actually "happening in the world". This is because all humans have their own preconceptions. If we see everything through "bias" or "negative thinking", we will only see sorrow in our lives. However, if we can channel positive thinking into what we see, then we will start to witness a happy and beautiful world.

The Better Man

The unpredictability of human nature affects everyone. You cannot judge a book by its cover is a proverb which has been proven true over and over again. Someone might be good-looking, but they could have a tainted heart. Likewise, someone could very well be quite ugly, but on the inside have a heart of gold. In almost every situation in daily life, someone is disappointed and someone is happy; someone faces sadness at every turn, while another experiences happiness every minute. Knowing how to have correct thoughts and the right frame of mind are key to happiness and this book provides vital guidance on how to be happy and avoid being downhearted.

Life is in your hand

This book reveals how to have a successful life or a tough life by outlining the ways in which people choose to do good or bad deeds in their life. All humans are different because we all have differing behavioral patterns. It is these patterns which influence our decision-making and thus our thoughts. If you want to know the secret of how to live a happy life, simply open this book and read the contents.

Money is not Everything

It is undeniable that money plays a very important role in the life of every human being. At first, money was invented for easy trade, exchange and barter. But as people amassed increasing wealth, these riches turned them from angels into devils who would do anything to obtain more. This book will open your eyes to the fact that although money can buy almost anything, it cannot buy you everything.

Damrong Pinkoon Company Limited

999 Gaysorn Plaza 5th Floor, Ploenchit Road, Lumpini, Pathumwan, Bangkok, 10330 Thailand

Tel: +66 88 96 55 699

Email: pinkoon123@gmail.com Instagram : pinkoon1

www.facebook.com / DamrongPinkoon_English

40 IDEAS FOR POSITIVE THINKING

ISBN :	978-616-374-305-3
Graphic Designed by	Damrong Pinkoon
Book Cover Designed by	Damrong Pinkoon
Written by	Damrong Pinkoon
Published by	Damrong Pinkoon
Ms. Sirisara Pinkoon	**for all the support**
Ms. Daranee Rattanathum	**for assisting**
Mr. Charlotte Woo	**for translation**
Mr. Philip Hall	**for editing**
Ms. Tanatta Tilokawichai	**for assisting**
Ms. Sukanya Taphun	**for assisting**
Ms. Wipapan Kongkow	**for assisting**

Special thanks for everything
I've learned from all my professors.
And to the great writers who wrote great books,
thank you for making it all possible for me.

TOPICS: 1. SELF-HELP

2. SELF IMPROVEMENT

3. SMART THINKING

4. INSPIRATION

5. PERSONAL DEVELOPMENT

40 IDEAS FOR POSITIVE THINKING

UK 1st Print in April 2015
Available in

United Kingdom	Brazil
India	Malaysia
South Korea	Czech
Hong Kong	Singapore
Columbia	Turkey
Phillippines	Brunei
France	Hungary
Lebanon	Italy
Netherlands	Russia
Indonesia	Costa rica
Mexico	Peru
Chile	Argentina
Germany	Canada
Paraguay	El Savador
Guatemala	Ecuador

Kindle Application
ebook : Amazon Application
www.Amazon.com
search : *Damrong Pinkoon*

Nook Application
ebook : Barnes & Noble Application
www.barnesandnoble.com
search : *Damrong Pinkoon*

Damrong Pinkoon Application
ebook : Damrong Pinkoon Application
iPad + iPhone + Google Play + Android
Search : *Damrong Pinkoon*

DAMRONG
PINK(OO)N

Contact **Damrong Pinkoon**
Email: pinkoon123@gmail.com
Email : pinkoon1@gmail.com
facebook / DamrongPinkoon_English

40

Ideas

for

POSITIVE

THINKING

Damrong Pinkoon